MONEY

KEITH TONDEUR

CWR

CONTENTS

INTRODUCTION

As I begin to write this study guide, the world appears to be in financial meltdown. Banks are being bailed out by the governments of many countries and the prospects probably look bleaker than at any time for the past seventy years.

Governments, lenders and personal borrowers all share the blame; greed overtook us and we somehow believed that we could borrow our way to a continually better future.

Did you know that somewhere in the world today, a child under the age of five is dying of hunger *every two seconds*? And this has been happening whilst we in the West have been spending so recklessly – buying things we have no real need of. In Britain alone the amount of personal debt has been increasing by £1 million every five minutes and we now have 15 million more credit cards in this country than we do people.

So, how are we as Christians supposed to respond? Do we take the teaching of Jesus seriously? In the Bible there are around 2,350 verses on handling money and possessions (compared to around 500 each on prayer and faith!), yet it is a subject we rarely hear about from the pulpit. Shockingly, the amount of debt we have and the giving we do is not that different from everyone else.

Jesus tells us that we belong to another kingdom and that we should have radically different priorities because of what He has done for us. He encourages us not to store up treasure on earth but to invest in eternity because we will have for ever to be glad we did! Yet, many of us get so caught up with materialism and advertising pressure that we forget godly priorities.

Today millions of people – including, sadly, many Christians – are suffering because they have been seduced by temporary worldly desires. Charities are struggling as giving is sacrificed before lifestyle; yet, if we were only to follow God's blueprint for our finances, we would be both healthier and happier.

Hopefully, this *Life Issues* study guide will help many understand the basics of God's teaching about money, enabling decisions to be made that bring freedom in this life, and eternal treasures in the next.

HANDLING MONEY GOD'S WAY

To open with

Can you remember what it felt like as a brand-new Christian? Share testimonies.

> *God's kingdom is like a treasure hidden in a field for years and then accidentally found by a trespasser. The finder is ecstatic – what a find! – and proceeds to sell everything he owns to raise money and buy that field. Or, God's kingdom is like a jewel merchant on the hunt for excellent pearls. Finding one that is flawless, he immediately sells everything and buys it.*
> (Matt. 13:44–46, *The Message*)

Direct impact

Jesus, the Son of God, died for us so we can have the certain hope of eternal life! This is the most priceless experience on earth, yet it is also a free gift to those who believe. Jesus willingly takes all our imperfections so that we are spotless and perfect in God's sight.

Compared to this, riches on earth are meaningless and inconsequential. Compared with eternity, the time we spend on earth is but a blink of an eye. However, whilst we are on earth we are God's hands – and also His wallet. And He challenges us to show the world His priorities.

'... if you have not been trustworthy in handling worldly wealth, who will trust you with true riches?' (Luke 16:11).
'You cannot serve both God and Money' (Matt. 6:24).
'... any of you who does not give up everything he has cannot be my disciple' (Luke 14:33).
'What good will it be for a man if he gains the whole world, and yet forfeits his soul?' (Matt. 16:26).

These verses can make us all feel uncomfortable! Yet it's clear that the way we handle money has a direct impact both on our spiritual life on earth, and also on the treasures we take with us to heaven.

By handling money and possessions in accordance with biblical principles we will be following Jesus more closely and will therefore have a more intimate relationship with Him. This is clearly shown in the parable of the talents. Those who handled their master's finances faithfully received his congratulations: 'Well done, good and faithful servant! You have been faithful with a few things; I will put you in charge of many things. Come and share your master's happiness!' (Matt. 25:21).

The way we handle money can move us either closer to, or further from, both God and other people. Sadly, money is often seen as a worldly issue and kept at arm's length by many Christians.

- Are you as open to praying about how to handle money and possessions as you are about other matters?
- As Christians, we tend to feel guilty if we've got money, and equally guilty if we haven't. Why do you think that is?

 Christ the King

During the Crusades in the twelfth century, mercenary soldiers were asked to fight. As it was a religious war they were ordered to be baptised but many mercenaries, as they were put under the water, held their swords out of it because they wanted to be in control of their most important possession. Today many of us behave in exactly the same way. We hold our wallets and purses tightly and tell God that He can be Lord of the rest of our lives, but that money is too important to surrender.

There is not good and bad in money – there is good and bad in people. We can use money for godly or selfish purposes, and the way we handle it shows very clearly where our priorities lie. It also accurately reflects our inner character.

It is impossible to enthrone Christ as King if we have not first dethroned all other gods, including our selfish love of money and possessions. From this we can clearly see that there is a strong connection between our spiritual state and the way we handle money. In fact, it can be argued that changes in our financial behaviour can demonstrate real spiritual growth (see Luke 19:1–9).

- If the rich young ruler (Mark 10:17–25) and the widow (Luke 21:1–4) attended Christian conferences, which do you think would be appearing on the platform?

 Master

Many Christians will handle more than £1 million in their lifetime! How many things have we purchased that we didn't really need? How much has advertising influenced us? How much have we wasted? This is important, given that we generally throw away *one-third* of our food in Britain. But the aim here is to focus on new and positive questions. What can we do for the poor? How can we use money that will literally make a difference to eternity?

In the Bible there are over 250 names for God, but when it comes to handling money and possessions His key title is 'Master'. It is essential, as we begin to change our money habits, to acknowledge that God owns everything: 'The earth is the LORD's, and everything in it, the world, and all who live in it' (Psa. 24:1). Recognising that God owns absolutely everything is the key element in allowing Jesus to become Lord of our money and possessions because it makes a complete difference to the way we think and act. From this point, every spending decision becomes a spiritual decision because we are no longer wondering how we are going to spend *our* money, we are praying, 'Lord, what do You want me to do with *Your* money?'

In 1 Timothy 6:8 we are told: 'But if we have food and clothing, we will be content with that.' We can rest assured that God has promised to supply all our needs – which are basically food, essential clothing and shelter. Anything over and above that is a 'want'. The trouble is, over the years we have constantly redefined what our needs are so they have become a much-expanded list! Still, God loves us and may well give us many of our wants as well, if He thinks they will genuinely benefit us and we will be good stewards of them. He is a generous God!

◎ Think

Many of our financial pressures and stresses come as a direct consequence of having not allowed God to be Lord of our finances. Acknowledging His role and being obedient should lead to both financial contentment and peace of mind. But to live like this in a society that tells us 'we are what we own' means developing a new mindset. Here are a few suggestions.

- Pray daily for a willingness to acknowledge that God owns everything – especially items you know you're attached to!
- Meditate on 1 Chronicles 29:11–12: 'Yours, O LORD, is the greatness and the power and the glory and the majesty and the splendour, for everything in heaven and earth is yours. Yours, O LORD, is the kingdom; you are exalted as head over all. Wealth and honour come from you; you are the ruler of all things.'
- See how long you can go without using the words 'my' or 'mine'!
- Every time you buy something, acknowledge that it belongs to God; if it is an asset, add it to your 'Surrender to God' list on page 12.

By surrendering our finances to God we will benefit in the following ways:

- We will never need to hoard money. God will clearly direct any savings and stop us trying to find security in our finances.
- We will neither overindulge and waste money, nor hold back on things that God tells us that we should or could have.
- Our financial position will never be allowed to boost or deflate our egos.
- We will never be in a place where money attempts to corrupt us through greed, pride or deceit.
- We will never need to worry about our financial position because God is providing what He knows we need.

Discuss

- Can a materialistic world ever be won over by a materialistic Church?
- 'When the Bible refers to money as power it does not mean something vague or impersonal ... No, according to Jesus and all the writers of the New Testament behind money are very real spiritual forces that energise it and give it a law of its own. Hence money is capable of inspiring devotion.'[1] Do you believe money is 'a power'?
- What dangers does having money bring – and what potential?
- Can people find true security in money?
- Does having more money and possessions increase or decrease anxiety? Why?
- Why is it hard to trust God with money?

◎ Prayer

Lord, we love You and thank You for all that You have done for us, and all the blessings You continually pour out on us. We ask that You will help us handle money Your way, and begin to grasp how dangerous it can become both spiritually and practically when we fail to do so. Amen.

◎ Practical step

Write a 'Surrender to God' list of all of 'your' assets (including house/cash/pensions etc.). Then pray: 'Today, Lord, I acknowledge that You own everything, including this list of assets. From now on, I want to ask You how to handle them. Please give me the power to do this. I trust that You have perfect plans for my life. Amen.'

Add to your list anything you feel God is telling you to buy in the future. You might like to write the prayer down in a journal, attach the list and add the date and your signature. (If you're married, you may wish to do this with your partner.)

GOOD STEWARDSHIP

◎ To open with

What is your definition of stewardship? Do you think the Church in the West generally reflects good stewardship regarding finances?

You made him ruler over the work of your hands; you put everything under his feet. (Psa. 8:6)

◎ Living generously

Having recognised that God is the owner of all things, we now need to consider our response. The word that best defines our role is 'steward'. In the Bible, a steward is given great responsibility. As stewards, we currently have full responsibility for all our Master's possessions!

Primarily, Christian stewardship is about challenging our attitudes regarding money and things. We have a simple choice of putting God first, or money and possessions. It's not easy to deal with a faith that, as it deepens, challenges us to ask fundamental questions about where we put our trust and look for security. But it is essential we face these issues head on if we really want to grow as Christians. In effect, it means we have to put Jesus' teaching into practice.

So Christian stewardship is a lifetime commitment to *living generously*, putting others' needs before our wants, and really caring. It is:

- Praising God for all His creation.
- Regarding our lives, money and possessions as gifts from God to be used in His service and for His glory.
- Viewing the earth's riches as precious gifts to be used wisely for all humankind.
- Being a responsible part of Jesus' mission to our hurting world.

Jesus tells us to hold on to things lightly. If we do this, we can begin to live in a new freedom. And once we come to that place, if we feel God is asking us to give something away – even something that means a lot to us – we can do it with the confidence that He has perfect plans for our lives; if He tells us to share with others, we can do so without question. (Incidentally, if we feel He is telling us to keep it all for ourselves then I suggest we haven't heard from God!) Jesus was both open-hearted and open-handed to all the people He met with needs. We should try to echo this. Each one of us is answerable to Him for how we live, our priorities, the choices we make and how we handle His finances and possessions.

- Micah 6:8 says: 'And what does the LORD require of you? To act justly and to love mercy and to walk humbly with your God.' Spend a couple of minutes meditating on this verse. Ask are *you* doing what the Lord requires of you when it comes to money and possessions?
- Read Luke 16:19–31. Lazarus is to be found in our world today. Sometimes we get a glimpse of him on a street corner, or on the TV screen. How will you respond?

◎ Eternal values

As Christians we have received many good things, and the most important is, of course, eternal life.

Jesus tells us, 'Do not store up for yourselves treasures on earth, where moth and rust destroy, and where thieves break in and steal. But store up for yourselves treasures in heaven, where moth and rust do not destroy, and where thieves do not break in and steal. For where your treasure is, there your heart will be also' (Matt. 6:19–21).

No earthly treasure is safe; there are no pockets in a shroud. When Nelson Rockefeller – supposedly the richest man who had ever lived – died, a journalist said to Rockefeller's accountant, 'Tell us what he left.' The reply is classic: 'He left all of it.'

Even if something can stand the test of time on earth it cannot stand the test of eternity. But Jesus is giving us a wonderful opportunity – the chance to exchange earthly, temporary goods for rewards that will be with us for ever. Surely as Christians our whole life strategy needs to be based on these eternal values. As the recent 'credit crunch' has shown, the only safe place to invest is in the kingdom of heaven. Everything else will be worthless at our death or Christ's return.

Therefore, good stewards withdraw money from their earthly accounts so that they can be credited in their heavenly accounts. They don't just plan ahead; they think an eternity ahead.

So how do we store up these eternal treasures? It is very simple – just do what our Lord did. Feed the hungry, clothe the naked, talk to a stranger and give time to lonely, lost and hurting people. Imagine the joy of entering heaven and having people rush up to you saying, 'I was hungry but you fed me!', 'I was lonely and you cared!' or 'It's only because of your faithfulness that I'm here!'

- Anything not connected to eternity is trivial, temporary and insignificant. Do you agree or disagree with this statement? Why/Why not?

◎ Opposing masters

By now, I hope you can see the benefit and feel the excitement that being a good steward brings!

Jesus actually implores us to grasp this as it has eternal consequences. In Luke 16:11 we read '... if you are untrustworthy about worldly wealth, who will trust you with the true riches of heaven?' (NLT). Luke 14:33 is even blunter: '... any of you who does not give up everything he has cannot be my disciple.'

It is very easy to justify certain behaviour, but we need to remember that even if we have worked hard and are earning substantial amounts it is *God* who has given us the 'talents' to do so. In fact, the more He has given us, the more responsibility we have to ensure that sound stewardship is carried out.

Remember, money is a power. When money speaks, truth is often silent. When we are not obedient stewards, when money comes first in our lives and becomes our master, we are likely to do things that will hurt others, even if this is only by neglect. But what is more important – money and possessions or people made in the image of God? Jesus tells us that we cannot serve both God and money (Matt. 6:24) because they are opposing masters.

It is essential that when we say 'Jesus is Lord' He is Lord of *all* our life and we haven't left our bank accounts out of this statement.

◎ Think

Here are some helpful tips on good stewardship.

- Keep an eye on where the money goes by developing a budget. (We will look at this practical step in the next chapter.)
- When you think you want something, ask God first – and wait for an answer!
- Eat sensibly and avoid waste.
- Learn to enjoy things without owning them. Renting, sharing and swapping things you need are good ways of using things and not letting them use you.
- If something is becoming a 'god' by taking over a part of your life or becoming a status symbol, seriously consider giving it away.

Sadly, in Britain many Christians have not fulfilled their roles as good stewards. It is so easy to overvalue material prosperity and underestimate or even take for granted the many blessings our wonderful Father has already bestowed upon us.

Under stewardship, possessions are not evil, or a right – they are a responsibility. We give not because we have to, or to get more in return, but because we simply love God and want to see His kingdom come and His will be done. We need to spend prayerfully and responsibly. It is only Jesus who can help both inspire and challenge us to reach out with money and things in love and compassion, with contentment in our hearts. If we say we have faith in Him but feel anxious about finances or possessions, then we still have a long way to grow.

A definition of a rich person is someone who has more money than we do. God is not asking us to live like the poorest people on earth. However, He *is* asking us what sort of stewards we are going to be, given the existence of so many *really* poor in our world. This is an individual choice but it has eternal ramifications.

Discuss

- How might we teach our children the principles of good stewardship?
- William Wilberforce said that when Christians stop thinking about the next world they become completely ineffective in this one. What do you think he meant by this?
- What could your local church do to practise better stewardship?
- What do you think deflects you from trying to store up treasures in heaven?
- What practical steps can you take today that will improve your stewardship of God's resources?
- If someone asked you how much you earned, how would you feel? Would you tell them? Why/Why not?

◎ Prayer

Lord, please forgive us when we handle money and possessions selfishly. Help us see clearly all the blessings You have poured upon us. Let us also see the needs of others with Your eyes. Especially, Lord, we want to thank You that because of Jesus we can look forward to eternity with You. Please help us have right priorities; help us to hold on to all things lightly. Show us ways that will benefit those in need on earth as we store real treasure in heaven. Amen.

◎ Practical step

Think about how you could be a better steward. Discuss this with your partner, if you are married. Look at the list you made of 'your' assets last week. How could these assets be better utilised, both for your own use and for the benefit of others? Could more be used to help the poor – your church, a charity, a project, a person known to you? Determine to pray about this, and seek God's will.

A MATERIALISTIC WORLD

◎ To open with

Think about some of the advertisements you have seen recently on TV. Are there any 'good' adverts, or particularly 'bad' ones? Discuss.

> *[Jesus] said to them, '... Be on your guard against all kinds of greed; a man's life does not consist in the abundance of his possessions.' And he told them this parable: 'The ground of a rich man produced a good crop. He thought to himself, "What shall I do? I have no place to store* my *crops." Then he said, "This is what* I'll *do. I* will tear down *my barns and build bigger ones, and there* I *will store all* my *grain and* my *goods. And* I'll *say to* myself, 'You have plenty of good things laid up for many years. Take life easy; eat, drink and be merry.'" But God said to him, "You fool! This very night your life will be demanded from you. Then who will get what you have prepared for yourself?" This is how it will be with anyone who stores up things for himself but is not rich towards God.'* (Luke 12:15–21, author's emphasis)

◎ Guiding principles

It is so easy to get caught up in self, but as we look at the self-centred words in the parable above, we can see that this is nothing new. Where we live, the car we drive, how we dress and the holidays we have seem all-important, judging by the constant stream of adverts urging us to 'better ourselves'. We really are the centre of our own universe. But as Christians we need to live radically different lives.

There are no verses in the Bible specifically instructing us how much we should earn or where we should live. But there are some very useful guiding principles. The key issue for us as Christians today is extracting ourselves from our materialistic society. Materialism, as its name indicates, is money-and-thing-centred and should therefore have no place in a Christian's life. However, there is also a danger in seeing money as evil and that somehow the less you have the more spiritual you are. As we have noted before, there is neither good nor bad in money. There is, however, good and bad motivation in all of us. We can use money to supply our own wants, or others' needs. We need to remember that it is the *love* of money that is 'a root of all kinds of evil' (1 Tim. 6:10).

- How do you feel about this statement: 'There are two ways of getting enough, one is to keep accumulating hoping that one day you may be eventually satisfied; the other is to desire less'?
- Read Philippians 4:12. Ask yourself: 'Am I learning to be content and not constantly desiring more?'

◎ Foolish!

You do not need to have money already to be a materialist; you just need to *want more*. The words 'my' and 'mine' sound innocent enough until we realise that they have seeped into our faith – some of us constantly seek personal blessings.

Over the past few decades the meaning of life in Britain has seemed to depend on ever-increasing status, money and power. We buy lottery tickets to get rich quick, watch quiz shows where the successful can win a million, and shop until we drop. And after all, why not? We're 'worth it', aren't we? We need to move from a bedsit to a one-bedroom flat to a three-bedroom semi-detached to a detached five-bedroom executive mansion. Our transport needs to go from a bicycle to a BMW and our holidays from a weekend at the seaside to anything – except another weekend at the seaside.

But the more things we have, the more time, money and effort it takes to maintain those things. Not only does this mean that we have less time to spend with God and other people but we are likely to worry that we could lose the things that matter to us.

Materialism is foolish! Earlier we read the words of Jesus in Matthew 16:26, 'What good will it be for a man if he gains the whole world, and yet forfeits his soul?', and thought about what is written in Luke 16:19–31. It is worth reading those verses again, for it is vital that we think long and hard about this story of the rich man and Lazarus. We need to remember that in worldly terms many of us fit into the 'rich' category. After the rich man died he realised how selfish he had been, but it was too late to do anything about it. Likewise, we need to act *now*. The sacrifices we make will impact eternity but so will our over-indulgences.

Are our houses warm homes where our family feels loved and secure or are they simply statements about 'our' success? Some of our biggest houses are surrounded by fences so high that they are like prisons – except that they are to stop people breaking in rather than breaking out! Having said that, there is nothing wrong in having a large house – they are often needed for hospitality and house groups, for example – and God wants His people in every stratum of society. But where we should be is His call, not ours.

- Have we really prayed about where, and how, we should live?

◎ Another kingdom

It is so easy to covet what others have. Yet we need to remember that Paul tells us in Ephesians 5:5 that a covetous or greedy person is an idolater and has '[no] inheritance in the kingdom of Christ'. We probably need to remember that by the time we have attained what the people we envy have, they have moved on and purchased something else! Sometimes we may hear someone saying that life is unfair, that they haven't been given what they deserve; I'm very grateful indeed that God hasn't given me what I deserve – aren't you?

A person with £10 can be more selfish than a generous person with £10 million – it all depends on attitude. Some years ago, I bought a new sofa which I felt looked just right in the lounge. That night, during house group, someone spilled coffee all over it! I felt really sorry for my friend who was so embarrassed. But my other emotion taught me a lot about myself and my own attitudes.

As we saw above, in worldly terms we are *all* rich. In truth, we are not called by God to take a vow of poverty but we are told to take one of generosity. This means we must be careful not to hoard, live in opulence or fail to give and, if we own something that prevents us from putting God first, we should determine not to keep it. Even those who are very wealthy through hard work or intelligence only go wrong if they use riches for self-centred and excessive lifestyles rather than for God's work.

So, we do not have to say 'no' to money and things, but we need to say 'yes' to using them for God. We belong to another kingdom. Our values need to reflect godly values and will therefore be radically different from those currently prevailing in our land. The material 'thing' we cherish most cannot compare with Jesus and His teaching. What we may have to lay down in itself may not be bad – it might well be good – but when all is surrendered, Jesus offers us the best there ever can be and we need to grab it with both hands.

◎ Think

The world asks what someone owns. Jesus asks how it is being used. So our lifestyle needs to have an impact on non-Christians and demonstrate our love for God and each other. In doing this practically, the Body of Christ is making Jesus visible to a world that increasingly has no contact with Him.

To help us live truly Christian lifestyles there are some sound principles we can follow:

- Focus on eternity.
- Pray about all major spending decisions.
- Avoid saying 'If only' or postponing doing things for God.
- Try not to allow your lifestyle to cause others to stumble.
- Be brave! Ask yourself, 'How much is enough?'
- Live simply and avoid waste wherever possible.
- Look at how the disciples lived together, by reading the early chapters of Acts.
- Remember we are in a spiritual battle and can easily be tempted to use money and possessions selfishly.
- Avoid being like the world. Romans 12:2 tells us 'Do not conform … to the pattern of this world'. We need to overcome the power of manipulative advertising.

- Don't try to keep up with the neighbours!
- Practise, practise, practise living contented lives.

Remember we need to:

- Be obedient to God's Word – always choosing God, people and eternity before money, possessions and the here and now.
- Be faithful and trust God with every aspect of our lives – including our finances.
- Demonstrate integrity in the way we live.
- By our actions, show Jesus to a world that lives selfishly. As rich people we can oppress the poor by greed or simply by neglect. It is not surprising, therefore, that Jesus is found on the side of the poor. So should we be.
- Show God's unconditional love to everyone He puts across our path.

When Jesus died for us on the cross, He was a naked man with no possessions. He had nothing but was giving everything. We were far more important to Him than money – or *anything*, as we can see when we read the account of His temptation by the devil (Matt. 4:1–11). He has made the ultimate sacrifice for us, but even small sacrifices we make today can have a huge impact on someone else's life.

◎ Discuss

- Look at these words of Benjamin Franklin: 'The eyes of other people are the eyes that ruin us. If all but myself were blind, I should want neither fine clothes, fine houses, nor fine furniture.'[2] Why do you think this is and why is 'keeping up with the neighbours' so important to many people?
- How do you think the consumerist society impacts on you? How about your church?
- What could it mean for you personally to live a truly Christian lifestyle in this materialistic world?
- What might be excessive when thinking about the house we live in, the car we drive or the clothes we wear?
- Do you think you would feel differently about biblical teaching on money and possessions if you lived in one of the poorest countries in the world?
- If you did live there, how do you think you might feel about Christians in the West?

◎ Prayer

Lord, please help us. We are bombarded with adverts telling us we need things when in reality we know that all we need is You. We want to honour You in the way we live, and develop Your priorities in our lives. Take the blinkers off us, Lord, and help us see the real need around us. Give us confidence to trust You completely so we handle money and possessions as You direct. Thank You, Holy Spirit, for guiding us in these matters. Amen.

◎ Practical step

Every Christian who is serious about both being a good steward and living a lifestyle honouring to God needs to draw up a budget. A budget simply tells us what money is coming in and where it is going. Without a budget, we might well be getting into debt without realising it. We will almost certainly be wasting money!

You, and your partner if you are married, could consider carrying notebooks around for two weeks to record *everything* you spend money on. Then you will be ready to prepare your budget, look at your priorities and start making all necessary changes. Contact Credit Action – www.creditaction.org.uk – for basic booklets or downloadable forms and further advice.

GIVING, DEBT AND SAVING

◎ To open with

Did you hear about the £50 note and the 50p coin talking in a bank? The £50 note said, 'I always go to hotels, health clubs or nice restaurants – when I'm not sitting here in the bank. How about you?' The 50p coin didn't have to think for long. 'I usually go to church,' he said. Puzzled, the £50 note replied, 'Church? What's church? I know I've never been there!' A funny joke – or a little too close for comfort?

As we work through all the biblical teaching on money, it is clear that we need to take action to help us demonstrate good stewardship and live our lives in a financially godly way. This has much to do with our priorities. Here we will be looking specifically at the responsibilities of giving, issues of debt, and saving.

◎ Giving

… Whoever sows sparingly will also reap sparingly, and whoever sows generously will also reap generously. Each man should give what he has decided in his heart to give, not reluctantly or under compulsion, for God loves a cheerful giver. And God is able to make all grace abound to you … You will be made rich in every way so that you can be generous on every occasion, and … your generosity will result in thanksgiving to God. (2 Cor. 9:6–11)

Firstly it is essential to see why God may give us more. It is so that we can be 'generous on every occasion'. Proverbs 11:25 tells us 'A generous man will prosper; he who refreshes others will himself be refreshed'. As we progress through life our income often increases significantly, but this is not for the purpose of raising our standard of living. Rather, it is to raise our standard of giving. Sadly, giving is often an afterthought rather than a priority. Giving says so much about us. If we give to a church or to a needy person it is a charitable act, but when we give cheerfully to the Lord *it is worship.*

It is also important to recognise that giving is not God's way of raising money – He can raise money any way He likes! Rather, it is His way of making us more like Jesus, who gave everything. Also, as we have seen, where our treasure is, our hearts will be; so, as giving becomes our lifestyle, we will draw closer to God. By now, we have learned that our giving impacts both earth and heaven.

Giving is much more about attitude than amount, which is why the story of the widow's offering in Luke 21:1–4 is so important. I believe that God does not look so much at what we give but rather at what we keep for ourselves – a very sobering thought.

It is clear from Malachi 3:10 that God expects everyone to tithe (give 10 per cent of their income), and in fact this verse is the only verse in the whole Bible where God asks us to test Him. I believe we should all try to aspire to this level of giving, but we do perhaps need to consider that in God's eyes 10 per cent is the starting point!

Generosity is a wonderful attribute but we will only be able to practise it when people are more important than possessions. Probably nothing is a clearer barometer of our commitment to Christ, our gratitude to Him and our concern for others than our financial commitment. A person committed with their chequebook is very committed indeed.

One verse that really helps with giving is 1 Corinthians 16:2: 'On the first day of every week, each one of you should set aside a sum of money in keeping with his income'. We can see from this that our giving should be:

- Periodic – 'On the first day of every week'
- Personal – 'each one of you'
- Priority – '… the *first* day' (author's italics)
- Planned – 'set aside … money in keeping with … income'

Matthew 25:40 tells us that when we give to the poor, lost and lonely we are giving to Jesus. When we don't, we are leaving our beloved Jesus hungry and naked (see Matt. 25:42–45). Giving is about sacrifice; it's about giving the best. Sacrificial giving involves saying goodbye to something we'd much rather keep.

- '... our income often increases significantly, but this is not for the purpose of raising our standard of living. Rather, it is to raise our standard of giving.' How does this statement challenge you?

Debt

> '... the borrower is servant to the lender.' (Prov. 22:7)

Anyone who has ever faced debt problems knows how true this statement is. The deeper we are in debt the more we become subject to the demands of those we owe money to. The freedom we had to use our finances in whatever way we chose has been taken from us. And debt produces every negative emotion we can think of – especially the fear of what is going to come through the post, or that the next phone call or ring of the doorbell will bring more bad news.

Unfortunately, over the past twenty years personal debt has become an epidemic in this country with the amount we personally owe growing by £1 million every five minutes, the total now being more than the Third World debt of Africa, Asia and Latin America added together. Debt cripples lives, and for many Christians has a negative impact on spiritual growth. At some stage in our lives nearly all of us will have to borrow money, usually for a house purchase. We need to ensure that we do not overcommit and expose ourselves and our families to risk – especially the risk of losing one's home. It's so easy to waste money on impulse buying.

Whenever we take out credit, or potential debt, we need to remember that we are assuming we will be able to repay this out of future income. God may have different plans for us! Look at the words of James 4:13–15: 'Now listen, you who say, "Today or tomorrow we will go to this or that city, spend a year there, carry on business and make money." Why, you do not even know what will happen tomorrow. What is your life? You are a mist that appears for a little while and then vanishes. Instead, you ought to say, "If it is the Lord's will, we will live and do this or that."' Debt can spring up on all of us very unexpectedly; for example, a sudden redundancy or illness can have a dramatic effect on our income. So we need to be very sensible in our financial commitments.

Debt creates huge rows between partners, and has many other negative effects on families. It can even lead, in desperate cases, to people taking their own lives as they lose all hope. But there are Christian organisations that can help – bringing both practical assistance and spiritual hope. These are listed at the end of this study guide.

Debt does need addressing. It will not just simply go away. Get help now!

• Ask yourself, 'Am I in denial about my true financial situation? Is my partner fully aware of where we stand?'

◎ Saving

In the house of the wise are stores of choice food and oil, but a foolish man devours all he has. (Prov. 21:20)

You might think that with all the emphasis on generous giving there would be nothing in the Bible about saving. In fact, we are encouraged to save to prevent us from ever being a burden to others.

The reasons for having savings are twofold: they can be used for the kingdom of God, and also for specific purposes in the future which would otherwise involve us going into debt. For example, we might save for our children's weddings, or to help them through university.

Debt puts pressure on the future, but savings make provision for tomorrow. Any saving means self-denial; there's always something the money could be spent on *today*! In the book of Genesis, we read that Joseph saved in the seven years of plenty so that when the seven years of famine arrived there was enough for all the nation (see Gen. 41). A great political move!

Rather like giving, saving is all to do with attitude. In 1 Timothy 6:9 we read: 'People who want to get rich fall into temptation and a trap and into many foolish and harmful desires that plunge men into ruin and destruction.' The motivation for saving has to be above reproach.

To make no provision for predictable times of need is foolish. But there is a clear difference between saving and hoarding. Saving means not relying on others to rescue us when we are without money; hoarding can mean seeking security in a bank account rather than in God.

- It's good to save for 'a rainy day', but all too easy to begin to find security in our savings rather than in God. What can we do to make sure we avoid this pitfall?

◎ Discuss

- Martin Luther said, 'There are three conversions, the conversion of the heart, mind and purse.'[3] Do you think we can ever feel comfortable about our level of giving?
- C.S. Lewis said, 'I do not believe one can settle how much we ought to give. I am afraid the only safe rule is to give more than we can spare.'[4] What implications does this have for us as Christians?
- Why do you think debt is so hard to talk about – especially to a partner?
- Are there things your church could do to help people in your community who have debt problems? For example, could someone train as a debt counsellor?
- Are any savings you have balanced by generous giving?
- If someone told you all your savings were gone, how would you feel?

◎ Prayer

Lord, we thank You for loving us so much. We thank You, too, for all the practical help we find in Your Word. As we work through our money issues involving giving, debt and saving, enable us always to have Your priorities in our hearts and minds. Help us, Lord, to rely on Your Spirit to guide us into making godly decisions. Further Your kingdom, we pray. Amen.

◎ Practical steps

- Evaluate your giving levels. What steps could you take this week to begin to share your possessions?
- If you are facing debt problems talk openly about them with your partner, if you are married, and then seek free and confidential help from either www.capuk.org or www.cccs.co.uk.
- If you have specific events to save up for in the future, work through your budget so you can start straight away.

◎ Conclusion

Whilst on this earth, we are God's money-managers. But how well are we doing the job? Are we handling our finances generally as God would like? At first glance, some of the biblical teaching on money seems hard. And yet, when we start applying it, we will find ourselves walking closer to God, and living freer lives.

Money can buy all the cosmetics in the world but it won't buy beauty. It can buy all the books in the world but not buy common sense. And money can never buy the greatest gift of all, because it is priceless – Jesus! Because of the gift of Jesus, we are cleansed, forgiven, totally loved and going to spend eternity with Him. There are millions who do not yet know His saving grace. Let's get storing up treasures in heaven right now!

Notes

1. Richard Foster, *Money, Sex and Power* (London: Hodder & Stoughton, February 2009).
2. See www.brainyquote.com
3. See www.thegracetabernacle.org
4. See www.thinkexist.com

Further Information

The following organisations provide further useful teaching and help:

Credit Action. For a range of basic money guides to be used in your community – www.creditaction.org.uk

Stewardship. For help with giving, but also a range of biblical materials for use in churches and of benefit to all Christians – www.stewardship.org.uk

Crown. For detailed courses looking at all aspects of biblical financial teaching – www.crownuk.org

Christians Against Poverty. For free debt counselling in your area – www.capuk.org

OTHER RESOURCES FROM CWR...

Other titles in the *Life Issues* series

Environment, Ruth Valerio
ISBN: 978-1-85345-481-3

Forgiveness, Ron Kallmier
ISBN: 978-1-85345-446-2

Relationships, Lynn Penson
ISBN: 978-1-85345-447-9

Time, Jani Rubery
ISBN: 978-1-85345-517-9

Work, Beverley Shepherd
ISBN: 978-1-85345-480-6

We currently have seven daily dated Bible reading notes. These aim to encourage people of all ages to meet with God regularly in His Word and to apply that Word to their everyday lives and relationships.

Every Day with Jesus – devotional readings for adults. ISSN: 0967-1889
Inspiring Women Every Day – for women. ISSN: 1478-050X
Lucas on Life Every Day – life-application notes. ISSN: 1744-0122
Cover to Cover Every Day – deeper biblical understanding. ISSN: 1744-0114
Mettle – for 14–18s. ISSN: 1747-1974
YP's – for 11–15s. ISSN: 1365-5841
Topz – for 7–11s. ISSN: 0967-1307

£2.49 each per bimonthly issue (except *Mettle*: £4.49 per four-month issue) from January 2009.

Get the benefit of Insight

The *Waverley Abbey Insight Series* gives practical and biblical explorations of common problems, valuable both for sufferers and for carers. These books, sourced from material first presented at Insight Days by CWR at Waverley Abbey House, offer clear insight, teaching and help on a growing range of subjects and issues.

Addiction: 978-1-85345-505-6
Anger: 978-1-85345-437-0
Anxiety: 978-1-85345-436-3
Assertiveness: 978-1-85345-539-1*
Bereavement: 978-1-85345-385-4
Depression: 978-1-85345-538-4*

Eating Disorders: 978-1-85345-410-3
Forgiveness: 978-1-85345-491-2
Perfectionism: 978-1-85345-506-3
Self-esteem: 978-1-85345-409-7
Stress: 978-1-85345-384-7

£7.99 each

*Released October 2009

Courses from CWR

We run a range of biblically-based training courses at our headquarters at Waverley Abbey House, Farnham, Surrey, England. These include courses on counselling and on life issues such as forgiveness.

For more details, call our Training Department on **+44 (0)1252 784700** or visit our website: **www.cwr.org.uk**

Prices correct at time of going to print.